A Zulu Family

A glossary of terms used in the text appears on page 28.

LIBRARY OF CONGRESS CATALOGING-IN-PUBLICATION DATA

McKenna, Nancy Durrell.
  A Zulu family.

  Previously published as: KwaZulu Africa. © 1984.
  Summary: Presents the life of an eleven-year-old Zulu girl and her family living in the homeland of Kwazulu in South Africa, describing the work of her relatives and neighbors, her chores and schoolwork, and her pride in her Zulu heritage.
  1. Zulus—Juvenile literature. 2. Kwazulu (South Africa)—Juvenile literature. [1. Zulus. 2. Family life—South Africa. 3. Kwazulu (South Africa)—Social life and customs. South Africa—Social life and customs] I. Title.
DT878.Z9M355 1986   968.4'9106   86-1
ISBN 0-8225-1666-7 (lib. bdg.)

Manufactured in the United States of America
  2 3 4 5 6 7 8 9 10 96 95 94 93 92 91 90 89 88 87

A Zulu Family

Nancy Durrell McKenna

Lerner Publications Company • Minneapolis

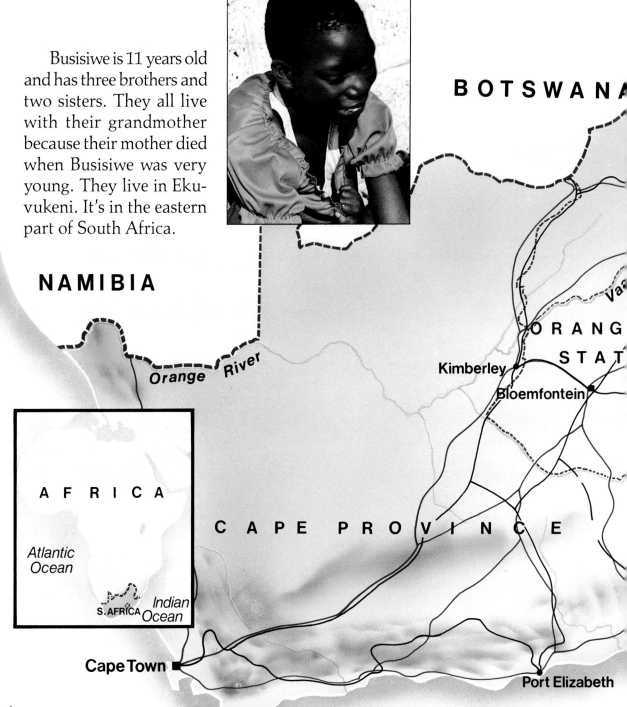

Busisiwe is 11 years old and has three brothers and two sisters. They all live with their grandmother because their mother died when Busisiwe was very young. They live in Eku-vukeni. It's in the eastern part of South Africa.

BOTSWANA

NAMIBIA

Orange River

ORANG

STAT

Kimberley

Bloemfontein

AFRICA

Atlantic
Ocean

S. AFRICA

Indian
Ocean

CAPE PROVINCE

Cape Town

Port Elizabeth

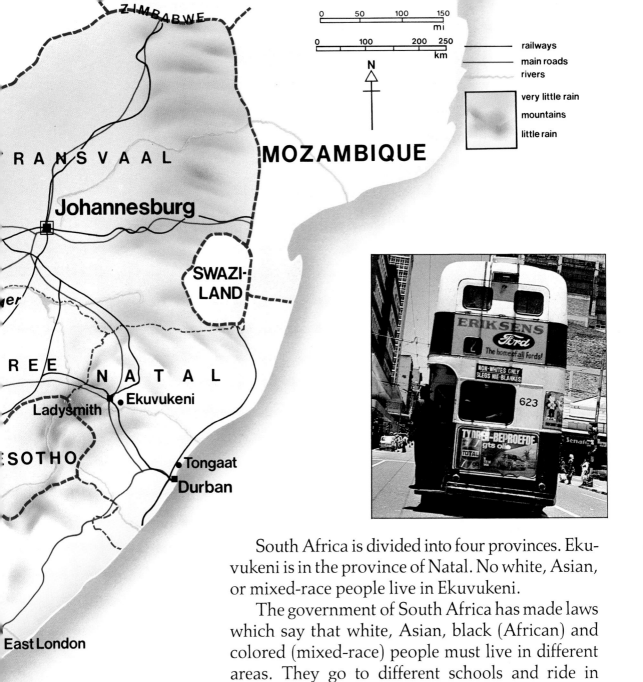

South Africa is divided into four provinces. Ekuvukeni is in the province of Natal. No white, Asian, or mixed-race people live in Ekuvukeni.

The government of South Africa has made laws which say that white, Asian, black (African) and colored (mixed-race) people must live in different areas. They go to different schools and ride in different cars on the trains. This system of keeping people apart is called *apartheid* (uh-PAR-tayt).

5

Busisiwe's grandmother's name is Thandiwe, which means "the loved one" in Zulu. Busisiwe and her family are Zulu people and speak Zulu as well as English. Thandiwe dresses in black because she is in mourning for her husband, Alfred. He died a year ago. He was an Anglican minister. Alfred preached on Sundays and during the week he visited people who were sick or needed help.

Thandiwe didn't always live in Ekuvukeni. She was born in a little village a short drive away, near the town of Ladysmith. Her parents were farmers.

Soon after she married Alfred, the government passed a law of resettlement. This law meant that Busisiwe's grandparents and many of their friends had to leave their homes and move to Ekuvukeni.

Thandiwe often tells Busisiwe about the day they had to move. A government truck came to take them very early in the morning. They had no time to pack. Thandiwe and her husband had to leave almost all of their things behind. When they were driven into Ekuvukeni, it seemed very dry and bare compared to the old village.

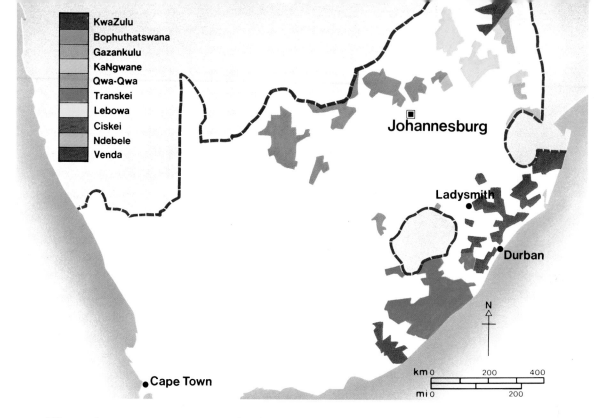

KwaZulu
Bophuthatswana
Gazankulu
KaNgwane
Qwa-Qwa
Transkei
Lebowa
Ciskei
Ndebele
Venda

Johannesburg

Ladysmith

Durban

N

Cape Town

km 0   200   400

mi 0   200

Ekuvukeni is in an area which the government calls KwaZulu. The government says that KwaZulu is a "homeland" where all Zulu people belong. Thandiwe says it isn't home for her. There are ten different "homelands" in South Africa. Each one is for a different group of African people.

When Thandiwe and Alfred first moved to Ekuvukeni, they lived in a house like this one, made of corrugated iron. This type of house gets very hot in summer and cold in winter.

After a few months, Busisiwe's grandparents built a mud house. Mud houses are much cooler in summer and warmer in winter. But when it rains, the mud begins to crumble and it's hard to keep repairing the walls.

There are different ways of building a mud house. One way is to dig mud from the ground and cut it into bricks. Another way is to make two wooden frames about the width of a fist apart. Then the gap is packed with mud and straw. Busisiwe's neighbors are building a house like this.

Busisiwe is very proud of the house the family lives in now. Her grandparents built it with some help from a neighbor. It is made of cement blocks, which cost a lot of money. Thandiwe and Alfred used money they had saved before they came to Ekuvukeni.

The house has a living room, dining room, two bedrooms and a kitchen, but the kitchen isn't finished yet. Busisiwe shares a bedroom with her sisters and aunt Florence. Thandiwe has a room to herself. There is no electricity in the house, so at night they use candles or oil-burning lamps.

Thandiwe's old mud house is just next door. It has two rooms. One room is used as a kitchen and Busisiwe's brothers sleep in the other.

Busisiwe's family has one of the best houses in Ekuvukeni. Many of their neighbors still live in houses made of mud or corrugated iron. Many of the men must live away from home to find work, so the women must manage on their own. They are too busy to build new houses and they can't afford to pay for builders or cement.

Jobs are hard to find in Ekuvukeni. There are no factories and the land is too dry and sandy for farming.

Some people manage to get jobs in Ladysmith. Busisiwe's neighbor, Mr. Zondi, works in a service station there. It takes about an hour and a half to get to Ladysmith by bus, so he has to get up at four in the morning. But it means he can live with his family.

Most of the men work much further from home. Busisiwe's uncle Sipho works on a sugar plantation near Tongaat. It is too far to travel every day, so he lives there most of the year.

Uncle Sipho carries a pass book which says that he lives in Ekuvukeni and is a farmworker in Natal. In South Africa, all Africans must have a pass book which says where they live and work.

Thandiwe has a pass book which says that she lives in Ekuvukeni. She has to take it with her everywhere, even if she's only going to the store.

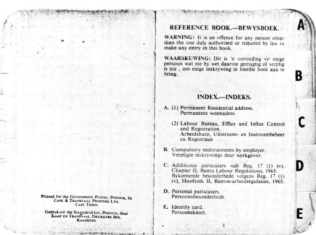

REFERENCE BOOK.—BEWYSBOEK.

WARNING: It is an offence for any person other than the one duly authorised or required by law to make any entry in this book.

WAARSKUWING: Dit is 'n oortreding vir enige persoon wat nie by wet daartoe gemagtig of verplig is nie , om enige inskrywing in hierdie boek aan te bring.

INDEX.—INDEKS.

A. (1) Permanent Residential address.
   Permanente woonadres.

   (2) Labour Bureau, Efflux and Influx Control and Registration.
   Arbeidsburo, Uitstroom- en Instroombeheer en Registrasie.

B. Compulsory endorsements by employer.
   Verpligte inskrywings deur werkgewer.

C. Additional particulars *vide* Reg. 17 (1) (v), Chapter II, Bantu Labour Regulations, 1965.
   Bykomende besonderhede volgens Reg. 17 (1) (v), Hoofstuk II, Bantoe-arbeidsregulasies, 1965.

D. Personal particulars.
   Persoonsbesonderhede.

E. Identity card.
   Persoonskaart.

Printed for the Government Printer, Pretoria, by
CAPE & TRANSVAAL PRINTERS LTD.
CAPE TOWN

Gedruk vir die Staatsdrukker, Pretoria, deur
KAAP EN TRANSVAAL DRUKKERS BPK.
KAAPSTAD

Busisiwe's father works on a construction site in Johannesburg, a big modern city in the province of Transvaal. It's a whole day's drive from Ekuvukeni, so he can't live with the family. He lives in Soweto, a township just outside Johannesburg. Most of the Africans who work in Johannesburg have to stay in townships like Soweto.

Busisiwe's father lives in a men's work hotel. He travels home once a year for Christmas. His family misses him a lot, but they need the money he sends them.

Every day, Busisiwe's father travels into the city by train. There are separate entrances to the train stations for black people and white people, and different cars on the trains. The station he goes through is always very crowded. Lots of people set up booths there to try to make a little money.

Busisiwe's father says that he can buy almost anything in the train station, from vegetables or live chickens, to pots to cook them in. He often buys food at the station on his way back from work.

Thandiwe says it is hard for her to look after the family with no men to help. Some of her friends go into Ladysmith to look for work in factories, but not many find jobs. Other women set up booths on the street to earn money. But many women have too much to do at home, especially when the men have to be away most of the year.

On weekdays, Thandiwe gets up at six A.M. to cook breakfast before the children go to school. They usually have mealie-meal, which is a kind of cornmeal mush. In Zulu, it's called *iphalishi* (if-ah-LISH-ee).

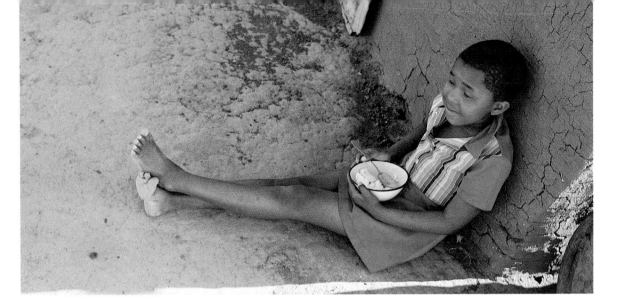

Busisiwe often eats iphalishi for dinner, too. Sometimes they have pumpkin pudding, and on extra-special days they have chicken. Meat is expensive, so they rarely eat it.

Thandiwe does all the shopping, mostly in the store in Ekuvukeni. If she wants something special, like clothes, she takes the bus to Ladysmith.

When Busisiwe isn't in school, she tries to help with the chores. Fetching water is her most important job. In good times, when there's been enough rain, they get water for cooking, washing, and drinking from a faucet outside their house. About four families share the faucet. Busisiwe's sister can carry a full bucket of water balanced on her head.

Summer in this part of South Africa is baking hot and very dry, and lasts from November until February. There never seems to be enough water. When there is no rain, the faucets dry up and the people in Ekuvukeni get their water from government water trucks. The trucks might come at any time of day or night, so they must always have their containers ready to fill.

Last year there was a drought where some of Thandiwe's friends live. Their faucets were dry for three weeks and they had to wait in line for water at a big reservoir. It took a very long time, because about five hundred people got their water there.

There are many other chores for Busisiwe to help with. In the morning, the women do their washing and housework. Then they collect wood for fires and light the braziers (grills) for cooking.

Some of the women plant vegetables on their plots of land. Where they used to live, there was enough land to plant mealies (corn) and sweet potatoes, as well as to keep animals.

A few of Busisiwe's neighbors planned to start new farms in Ekuvukeni, so they brought along their farm tools and machines. But there isn't enough land in Ekuvukeni for farming, and the soil is too dry and sandy.

Thandiwe has organized a group with ten other women. They meet at Busisiwe's house every week and teach each other new skills, like crocheting or making school uniforms. Last year they set up a workshop to repair bicycles and primus stoves (camp stoves).

Busisiwe goes to school in Ekuvukeni, about fifteen minutes' walk from her house. School starts for her at 8 A.M. and ends at 1 P.M. There isn't enough room in the school for everyone to attend at the same time, so another class has lessons in the afternoon.

Busisiwe is in her fourth year in school. Her teacher writes the lessons on the board and the class repeats them out loud.

Busisiwe's favorite subject is nature study, but she is also learning Zulu, English, arithmetic, and health and hygiene.

It costs Thandiwe 15 rand a year to send Busisiwe to school. The school uniform is expensive, too. Busisiwe is glad that Thandiwe's work group can make her next uniform.

All Busisiwe's brothers and sisters go to school too, and she hopes to go on to secondary school. But many families in Ekuvukeni can't afford to send their children to school.

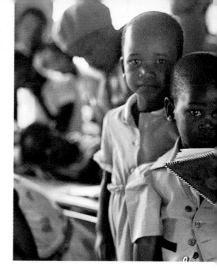

Sunday is a special day for Busisiwe's family. Her grandmother gets up very early and boils water for them to wash in. It's Busisiwe's job to wash her little sister's hair. Then they dress up for church.

When Busisiwe's grandfather was alive, he preached every Sunday. Now their church doesn't have its own minister. When they have a visiting minister coming to preach, Thandiwe irons a fresh gown for him so he will look just right.

The people in Busisiwe's church don't have their own building yet, so they use the secondary school. When there is no visiting minister, the men and women in the congregation take turns leading the service. Busisiwe loves singing hymns, and her grandmother knows all the words.

After church, Thandiwe stays to talk to her friends and find out all the news. Busisiwe is always happy to see her grandmother laughing and joking.

In the evening when it's dark and only the candles are lit, Busisiwe likes to hear her grandmother tell stories about her childhood, or about her and Grandfather Alfred when they were young.

Sometimes she tells about the history of the Zulu people and the great Zulu leaders, like King Shaka.

Busisiwe and her brothers and sisters are learning the cheers of the Zulu people. They take turns being the leader. Thandiwe and Aunt Florence are the audience. *"Amandla! Ngawethu!"* means "Power to the people!" Busisiwe's grandmother says that their father would be proud of them.

Glossary

Apartheid is a system which separates South African people into four groups: white (about 4,500,000 people); Asian (about 800,000 people); African or black (about 21,400,000 people); and colored or mixed-race (which includes all the people not in the other three groups, about 2,500,000 people). Apartheid also separates the African people into ten groups, based on the languages which they speak.

The apartheid system was set up after white settlers from Holland, and later from Britain, had slowly taken over the land by force, during a period of over 200 years.

In South Africa, white people have many privileges which the other groups of people do not have. Africans are not allowed to vote for the government and make the laws.

Homelands: In the early 1900s, the government set aside a number of areas and passed laws which said that African people must live only in these areas. Later, the government divided these areas into ten different groups which they called "homelands." African people do not use the word "homelands." Many people call these areas *"bantustans."*

The government divided the African people into ten groups, based on the different languages which were spoken. Each group was assigned to a different bantustan. KwaZulu is the bantustan for the people who speak the Zulu language. African people are not allowed to move out of their bantustans to live or work, without special permission in their pass books.

Pass book: All Africans over the age of sixteen must carry a pass book. It contains a photograph of the person and says where they are allowed to live and work.

It is against the law for an African to be without a pass book, or to go to areas which are not in his pass book. These regulations are called the pass laws.

Resettlement: When Africans are forced to move from areas which the government has set aside for white people, they are resettled in camps in the bantustans.

Townships: These are usually areas on the outskirts of big cities. Most of the Africans who work in the cities must live in townships. No white people live in the townships.

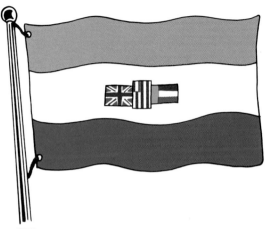

Facts About South Africa

Capitals: Cape Town (legislative), Pretoria (administrative), and Bloemfontein (judicial)

Official Languages: Afrikaans and English
Many Africans also speak a tribal language such as Zulu.

Form of Money: the rand

Area: 471,445 square miles (1,221,037 square kilometers)
This area is slightly larger than the area of Texas, New Mexico, and Oklahoma combined.

Population: about 32 million people.
About nine times as many people live in the United States as in South Africa.

EUROPE

A S I A

AFRICA

S. Africa

AUSTRALIA

31

Families the World Over

Some children in foreign countries live like you do. Others live very differently. In these books, you can meet children from all over the world. You'll learn about their games and schools, their families and friends, and what it's like to grow up in a faraway land.

AN ABORIGINAL FAMILY	AN ESKIMO FAMILY	A FAMILY IN MOROCCO
AN ARAB FAMILY	A FAMILY IN FRANCE	A FAMILY IN NIGERIA
A FAMILY IN AUSTRALIA	A FAMILY IN INDIA	A FAMILY IN PAKISTAN
A FAMILY IN BOLIVIA	A FAMILY IN IRELAND	A FAMILY IN PERU
A FAMILY IN BRAZIL	A FAMILY IN ITALY	A FAMILY IN SINGAPORE
A FAMILY IN CHILE	A FAMILY IN JAMAICA	A FAMILY IN SRI LANKA
A FAMILY IN CHINA	A FAMILY IN JAPAN	A FAMILY IN WEST GERMANY
A FAMILY IN EGYPT	A FAMILY IN LIBERIA	A ZULU FAMILY

Lerner Publications Company
241 First Avenue North
Minneapolis, Minnesota 55401